First World War
and Army of Occupation
War Diary
France, Belgium and Germany

66 DIVISION
198 Infantry Brigade
Headquarters
9 September 1915 - 20 February 1916

WO95/3138/1

The Naval & Military Press Ltd
www.nmarchive.com
Published in association with The National Archives

Published by

The Naval & Military Press Ltd

Unit 10 Ridgewood Industrial Park,

Uckfield, East Sussex,

TN22 5QE England

Tel: +44 (0) 1825 749494

www.naval-military-press.com

www.nmarchive.com

This diary has been reprinted in facsimile from the original. Any imperfections are inevitably reproduced and the quality may fall short of modern type and cartographic standards.

© **Crown Copyright**
Images reproduced by permission of The National Archives, London, England, 2015.

Contents

Document type	Place/Title	Date From	Date To
Heading	WO95/3138/1		
Heading	66th Division 198th Infy Bde Bde Headquarters Mar-Dec 1917		
Heading	66 Div HQ 198 Bde 1915 Sep-1916 Feb		
Miscellaneous	Monthly Statement In Connection With War Diary	04/09/1915	04/09/1915
War Diary	Pease Pottage	09/09/1915	20/09/1915
War Diary	Shoreham	20/09/1915	20/09/1915
War Diary	Cowfold	21/09/1915	21/09/1915
War Diary	Pease Pottage	22/09/1915	22/09/1915
War Diary	East Grinstead	23/09/1915	23/09/1915
War Diary	Tonbridge	24/09/1915	24/09/1915
War Diary	Burham Camp	28/09/1915	03/10/1915
War Diary	Burham	01/10/1915	31/10/1915
War Diary	Crowborough	03/11/1915	16/01/1916
War Diary	Hartfield	02/02/1916	02/02/1916
War Diary	Crowborough	04/02/1916	04/02/1916
Heading	War Diary of 198th Infantry Brigade From 1st February 1916 To 29th February 1916 Volume I		
War Diary	Crowborough	10/02/1916	20/02/1916

WO 95/3138/1

66TH DIVISION
198TH INFY BDE

BDE HEADQUARTERS

MAR – DEC 1917

66 DIV

HQ 198 BDE

1915 SEP — 1916 FEB

3026

198th Infantry Brigade.

MONTHLY STATEMENT IN CONNECTION WITH WAR DIARY.

Brigade.	198th Infantry Brigade.
Mobilization Centres.	Blackburn.) Burnley.) Lancashire. Ashton-u-Lyne.) Oldham.)
Temporary War Station.	Pease Pottage Camp, Crawley, SUSSEX.
Stations since occupied subsequent to Concentration.	Southport. Burgess Hill.) Haywards Heath.) Sussex. Cuckfield.)

(a) **Mobilization.**   Nil

(b) **Concentration at War Stations.**   The four units moved to Pease Pottage by Route March on the 26th June, 1915.

(c) **Organisation for Defence.**   Definite instructions not yet received.
    Ammunition. 300 rounds Japanese Ammunition per rifle.
    Machine Guns are arriving in parts.
    Signalling Apparatus arriving in parts.
    No Range Finders.
    Miniature Range now in working order.
    Musketry Course completed at Sandwich.

(d) **Training.**   Entrenching, Bayonet Fighting and Physical Training continuous. Musketry being carried on at the Miniature Range. Company Field Training has been carried out by Double Companies, under difficulties, throughout the month.

(e) **Discipline.**   Good.

(f) **Administration.**

    1. Medical Services.   Satisfactory.

    2. Veterinary Services.   Satisfactory.

    3. Supply Services.   Very Satisfactory.

    4. Transport Services.   Very weak up to date - inefficient for movement of Brigade. A serious deficiency of water-carts exists.
        Much improvement may be expected on receipt of harness, expected daily.

    5. Ordnance Services.   Satisfactory.

    6. Channels of Correspondence in Routine Matters.   Satisfactory.

    7. Range construction.   Miniature Range completed near camp.

    8. Remounts.   Improving.

(g) **Reorganisation of Home and Imperial Service of T.F.**   This will be a great improvement if carried out. At present there are in the Brigade some 80 men declared Medically fit for Home Service only by Standing Medical Board.

(h) **Preparation of Units for Imperial Service.**   The Brigade is reduced to a lamentable weakness owing to drafts.

Pease Pottage. 4-9-15

       Colonel
       Comdg 198th Infantry Bde.

Army Form C. 2118.

WAR DIARY
or
INTELLIGENCE SUMMARY

(Erase heading not required.)

Instructions regarding War Diaries and Intelligence Summaries are contained in F. S. Regs., Part II. and the Staff Manual respectively. Title pages will be prepared in manuscript.

Hour, Date, Place	Summary of Events and Information	Remarks and references to Appendices
9-9-15 Pease Pottage.	Received orders to nominate the following number of officers for 1st Line. Mediterranean Expeditionary Force. 2/5th Batt. East Lancs.Regiment. 1. 2/9th Batt. Manchester Regiment. 2.	
20-9-15. Pease Pottage.	Received orders to nominate the following numbers of officers for 1st Line. Mediterranean Expeditionary Force. 2/4th Batt. East Lancs. Regiment 3. 2/5th Batt. East Lancs. Regiment 14. 2/9th Batt. Manchester Regiment 11. 2/10th Batt. Manchester Regiment 9.	
8 am.20-9-15. Shoreham.	2/10th Batt.Manchester Regiment left Shoreham and marched to Cowfold.	
8 am.21-9-15. Cowfold.	2/10th Batt.Manchester Regiment left Cowfold and marched to Pease Pottage Camp.	
8 am.22-9-15. Pease Pottage.	The Brigade left Pease Pottage and marched to East Grinstead. into billets.	
23-9-15. East Grinstead.	The Brigade marched from East Grinstead to Tonbridge into billets.	
7 am.24-9-15. Tonbridge.	The Brigade left Tonbridge and marched to Burham Camp arriving at 4-50 pm. Lieut.General Woolcombe and the G.O.C., Division inspected the Brigade on the march.	
3 pm.28-9-15. Burham Camp.	The G.O.C., Division inspected the Brigade and Camp.	

Burham Camp,
3rd Oct.1915.

C. S. McInnes
Colonel,
Commanding 198th Infantry Brigade.

Army Form C. 2118.

WAR DIARY
or
INTELLIGENCE SUMMARY

(Erase heading not required.)

Instructions regarding War Diaries and Intelligence Summaries are contained in F.S. Regs., Part II. and the Staff Manual respectively. Title pages will be prepared in manuscript.

Hour, Date, Place	Summary of Events and Information	Remarks and references to Appendices
Oct.1st to Oct.24th Burham.	Brigade entrenching on Blue Bell Hill.	
Oct.4th.	The following officers proceeded to the Mediterranean Ex.Force:- 2/4th Batt. East Lancs. Regt. 3. 2/5th Batt. East Lancs. Regt. 8. 2/10th Batt. Manchester Regt. 9.	
Oct.6th. Burham.	Representative of the Munitions Department accompanied by A.Q.M.G., 2nd Army C.F. inspected the Brigade and called for volunteers for munition work.	
Oct.8th Burham.	Lieut.General C.L.Woollcombe C.B. (2nd Army) and Brig.General C.E. Beckett C.B., 66th (East Lancs.) Division inspected Burham Camp and the Brigade at work in the trenches.	
Oct.12th Burham.	Following officers proceeded to Mediterranean Ex.Force:- 2/9th Batt. Manchester Regiment 11.	
Oct.13th Burham.	Brigade Machine Gun Course completed - 1 Machine Gun section for each unit fully trained.	
Oct.25th Burham.	Brigade commenced move by road to Crowborough camp-by Units.	
Oct.31st Burham.	Move to Crowborough Camp completed.	

Crowborough,
3rd Nov.1915.

[signature]
Colonel,
Commanding 198th Infantry Brigade.

CONFIDENTIAL.

Army Form C. 2118.

WAR DIARY
or
INTELLIGENCE SUMMARY

(Erase heading not required.)

198TH INFANTRY BRIGADE.

Instructions regarding War Diaries and Intelligence Summaries are contained in F.S. Regs., Part II. and the Staff Manual respectively. Title pages will be prepared in manuscript.

Hour, Date, Place	Summary of Events and Information	Remarks and references to Appendices
2-11-15. CROWBOROUGH.	Transport of the Brigade Inspected by General LOGAN, 2nd Army, C.F.	
16-11-15 and 17-11-15. CROWBOROUGH.	Brigade Inspected by Major General E.T.DICKSON, Inspector General of Infantry.	
22-11-15. CROWBOROUGH.	Japanese Arms withdrawn from the Units of this Brigade AND .303 Arms issued to them.	
29-11-15. CROWBOROUGH.	Establishment of Officers reduced to 23 per Unit (War Office Letter 9/Infantry/2 (T.F.3) dated 8-11-15.)	

Crowborough,
3rd December, 1915.

[signature] Major
[signature] Colonel,
Commanding 198th Infantry Brigade.

Army Form C. 2118.

WAR DIARY
or
INTELLIGENCE SUMMARY

(Erase heading not required.)

Hour, Date, Place	Summary of Events and Information	Remarks and references to Appendices
10 a.m. 11th Dec: 1915. Crowborough	Inspection by G.O.C. 66th (2nd East) Division.	W2

Crowborough
4. i. 1916.

C. J. Morton Stevens Colonel
Commdg: 198th Infantry Brigade.

Army Form C. 2118.

WAR DIARY
or
INTELLIGENCE SUMMARY

(Erase heading not required.)

Instructions regarding War Diaries and Intelligence Summaries are contained in F. S. Regs., Part II. and the Staff Manual respectively. Title pages will be prepared in manuscript.

Hour, Date, Place	Summary of Events and Information	Remarks and references to Appendices
10 a.m. 16th Jany 1916 Crowborough.	The Brigade Major and one Commanding officer of unit proceeded to the Western Front on one weeks instructional tour.	A.I.h.
From 2nd Febry 1916 Hartfield	Inspection of 1st Line Transport by G.O.C. 66th (2nd East Lancs) Division on concentration march of Divisional 2nd line transport and Field Ambulances &c.	A.I.

Crowborough.
4th Feby. 1916.

A.S. Jackson Stewart
Colonel,
Commanding 198th Infantry Brigade.

CONFIDENTIAL

WAR DIARY

OF

198TH INFANTRY BRIGADE.

From.......1st February 1916.   To...29th February 1916.

VOLUME I.

WAR DIARY
or
INTELLIGENCE SUMMARY. Cyz.
(Erase heading not required.)

Army Form C. 2118.

Hour, Date, Place	Summary of Events and Information	Remarks and references to Appendices
16.2.16. Cromborough.	Colonel C.S. Prideaux Steward assumed Command of the 66th Territorial Division.	Cyz.
10 am 12.2.16. Cromborough.	Lieutenant Colonel W. Patterson, 9/16th Battn. Manchester Regt. assumed Command of the 198th Infantry Brigade.	Cyz.
20.2.16. Cromborough.	Capt. A.S. Butler, Staff Captain, left his Brigade to take up an appointment at the War Office.	Cyz.
	[signature] Lieut. for Colonel Commanding 198th Infantry Bde.	

www.ingramcontent.com/pod-product-compliance
Lightning Source LLC
Chambersburg PA
CBHW081517160426
43193CB00014B/2722